Copyright © 2025 by Jay Lyles
Illustrated by QBN Studios

All rights reserved. No part of this book may be reproduced in any form or by any electronic or mechanical means, including information storage and retrieval systems, without permission in writing from the publisher, except by reviewers, who may quote brief passages in a review.

My Grandparents and I

written by Jay Lyles
Illustrated by QBN Studios

It's the last day of school signaling for the year to be done,
You have done your best, passed every test, and now it's time for some summer fun.

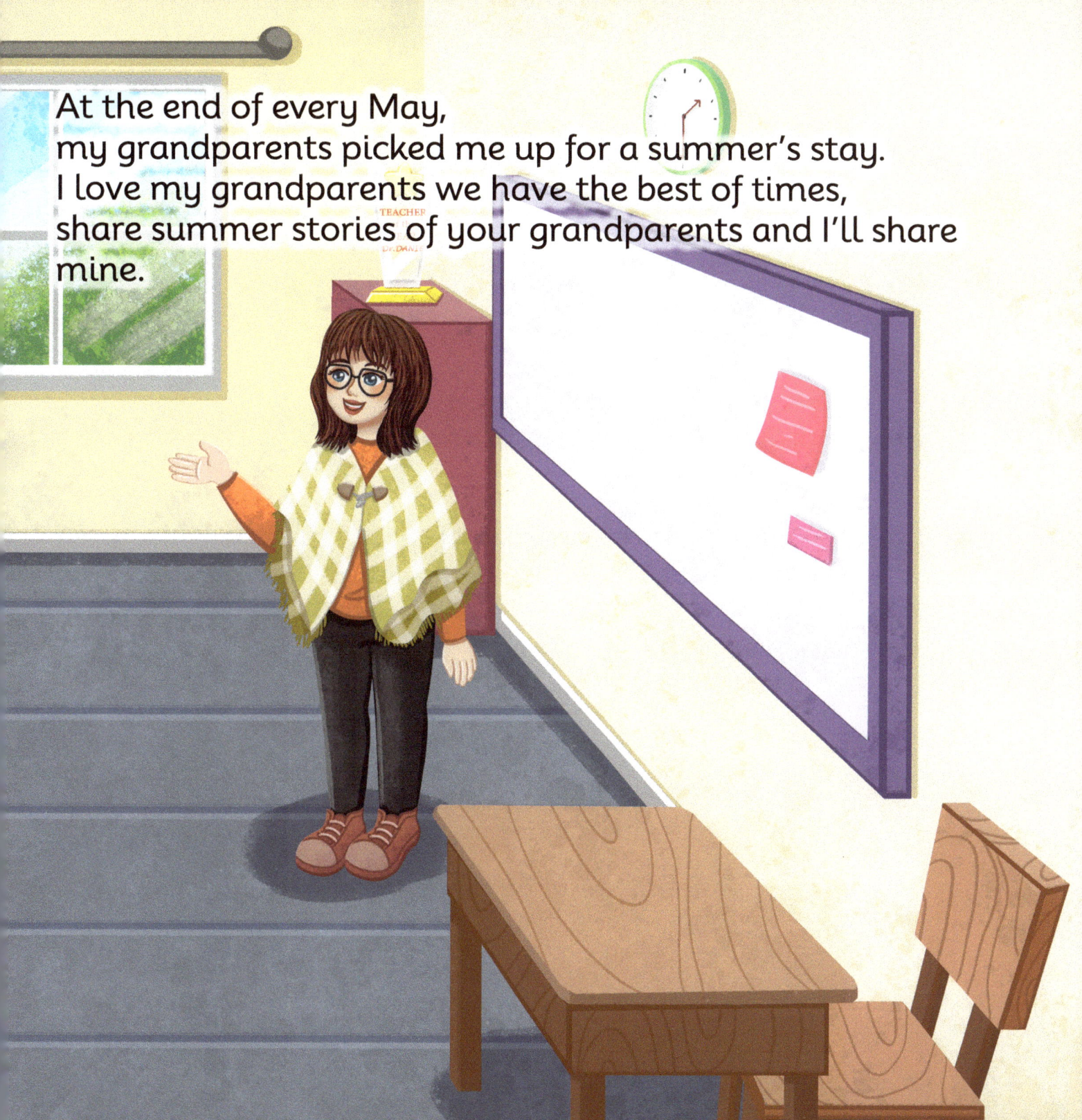

At the end of every May,
my grandparents picked me up for a summer's stay.
I love my grandparents we have the best of times,
share summer stories of your grandparents and I'll share mine.

My Grandma bakes cookies while Grandpa reads me a story.

Chocolate chips are my favorite to eat while listening to Grandpa tell tales about fighting for Old Glory.

Mi Abuela y Abuelo take me to the pool.

Mi Abuela sits under the umbrella and my Abuelo tries a dive, but only he thinks it is cool.

Memaw & I ride on a horse while Pawpaw tends to the field,

several acres of green pasture is a whole lot of ground to fill.

Granny and I help Granddad train for the Geriatric Games.

She is the coach and I'm attached to his back as weighted support keeping him on track.

Since we live so far away we don't always see each other on the Christmas holiday.

My Nana is so sweet and my Papa is so fly,
To make the time complete, we have Christmas in July.

I love it when Big Mama and Grandaddy take me to Sunday praise.

Big Mama and I sing a message of peace and we listen to Granddaddy preach.

Me and Nan go on a shopping spree,

hair, nails, and gifts all with Pop's money.

My Poppy and I don't know how to act,

We run through the house keeping GiGi up from her afternoon nap. Fed up with our play, she puts us outside for the rest of the day.

My Mum-mum is a Registered Nurse and Dad-dad is the patient telling us where it hurts.

We check his temp and bandage his wounds, and with a kiss on the cheek, we tell him to feel better soon.

Grandma and Grandpa take us to the community carnival, where we brawl for it all. We challenge Grandpa in a tug of war.

Wow, that's great! You guys are *FUNatic*, Now let me tell you some stories that are just as fantastic.

Before my dad there was Papa and Mummy, she was so sweet and he was so funny.

We would just laugh while chilling at the lake, floating along in the boat, times were so great.

Other times we would go full throttle,
With a flick of the gas, we would ride so fast
Nothing with them was impossible.

Now on my mom's side were Mimi and Papa, we were very close,

When it came to hockey and baseball we did the most.

"Yes, we did. Now it's your turn to make so many memories for all time to last.

These memories are precious and sometimes make me want to cry,

There was no funner time when it was
My Grandparents and I. "Goodbye!"

About the Author

Jermaine Lyles, AKA Jay the Author, is an educator, storyteller, and lifelong believer in the power of family traditions. Inspired by his childhood summers and the joy of multigenerational love, *My Grandparents and I* is a heartfelt tribute to the memories children create with their grandparents. Jermaine's writing blends rhyme, humor, and cultural diversity to reflect the many ways love shows up across generations. When he's not writing or teaching, Jermaine enjoys powerlifting, spoken word poetry, and sharing stories that make people smile, think, and remember the special bonds that shape who we are.

Books by Jay

Enjoy more delightful stories by **Jay Lyles**—each one crafted to spark imagination, laughter, and a love of learning:

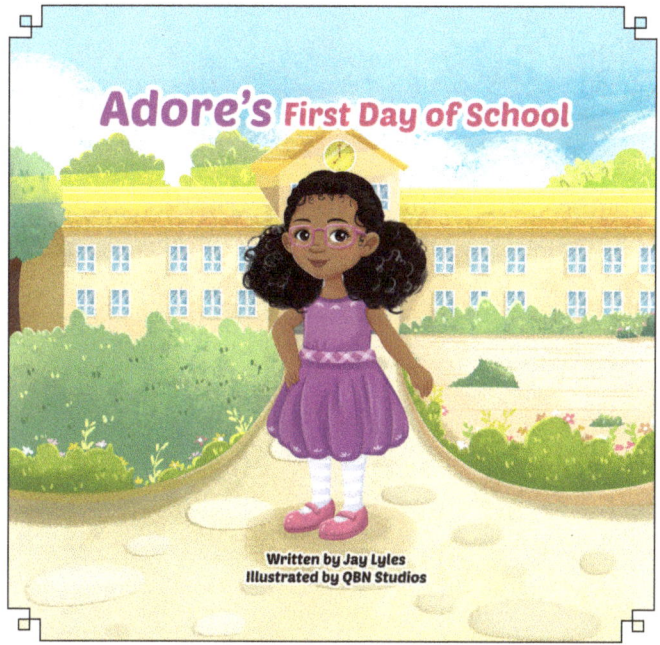

Adore's First Day of School

Follow Adore as she tackles her nerves and discovers the fun, friendship, and courage that come with starting something new.

ABCs of What I Want to Be

An A-to-Z journey through dreams and careers—encouraging children to imagine big and believe in themselves.

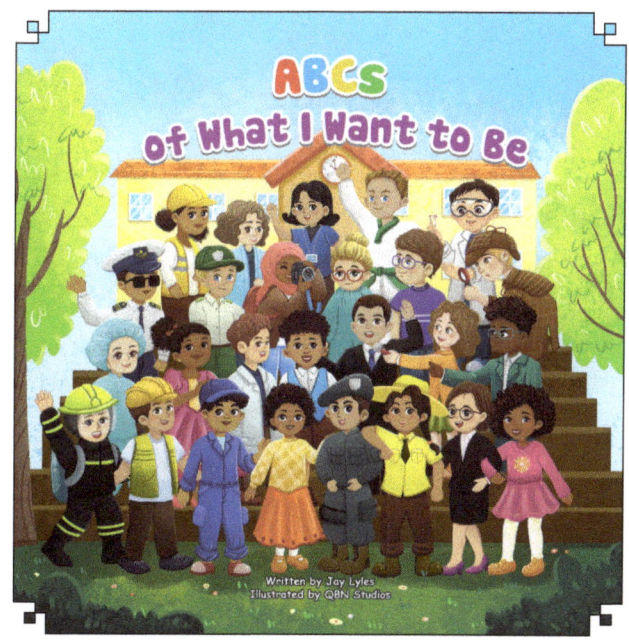

Jay the Jazz Playing Jaguar and His Jungle Friends

A jazzy, joy-filled adventure where jungle animals learn to groove together through friendship and music.

Galaxy the Gigantic Gorilla

Meet Galaxy, the not-so-scary giant gorilla with a heart of gold, who learns that being big means being gentle, too.

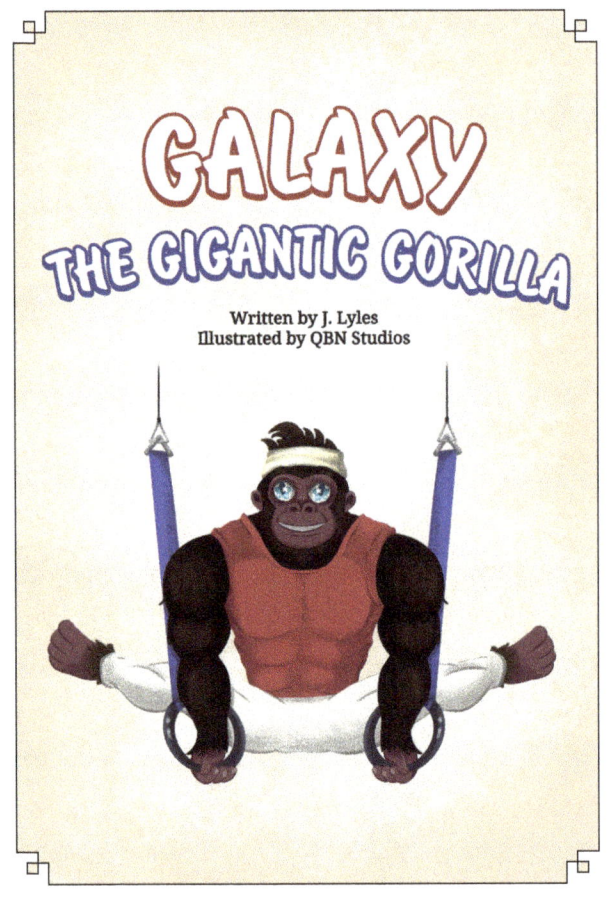